Arnold Schwarzenegger

Julia Holt

Published in association with The Basic Skills Agency

Hodder & Stoughton

A MEMBER OF THE HODDER HEADLINE GROUP

Acknowledgements
Cover: © PA Photos

*Photos: pp. 8, 15, 25 © Associated Press; pp. 13, 17, 24 © The Kobal Collection;
p. 26 © AP Photo/Albert Ferreira..*

Orders: please contact Bookpoint Ltd, 130 Milton Park, Abingdon, Oxon OX14 4SB.
Telephone: (44) 01235 827720, Fax: (44) 01235 400454. Lines are open from 9.00 – 6.00,
Monday to Saturday, with a 24 hour message answering service. Email address:
orders@bookpoint.co.uk

British Library Cataloguing in Publication Data
A catalogue record for this title is available from The British Library

ISBN 0 340 84870 7

Second edition. First published 1996
Impression number   10 9 8 7 6 5 4 3 2 1
Year   2007 2006 2005 2004 2003 2002

Copyright © 2002 Julia Holt

Typeset by SX Composing DTP, Rayleigh, Essex.
Printed in Great Britain for Hodder & Stoughton Educational, a division of Hodder
Headline Plc, 338 Euston Road, London NW1 3BH by The Bath Press Ltd.

Contents

1 Introduction

In 1997, they opened a museum
in the small town of Graz, in Austria.
It was the Arnold Schwarzenegger museum.
In it there are his old body-building machines.
He used them to build his biceps
to a huge 56 centimetres round.
He flew in to open the museum
in his own jet.

He said,
'I always dreamed of being a body-builder
and going to Hollywood but I never dreamed
I would make it this big.'

Arnold Schwarzenegger always dreamed of
making it big.

Arnold was right to be amazed.
His story is amazing.
How could body-building
be a ticket to a better life?
How could a man
with a strong Austrian accent
and no acting skills
become a top Hollywood star?

2   Growing Up

Arnold was born on 30 July 1947
in a small village, near Graz in Austria.
The family did not have a phone,
an inside toilet or a fridge
until Arnold was 14.

Arnold's father was a policeman
and he was strict.
Arnold and his big brother
got up at 6 a.m. to do jobs in the house.
Then they had to do 15 minutes of squats
and sit-ups before breakfast.
If Arnold went to the cinema,
he had to write an essay about it
when he got home.

Arnold's father wanted him
to be a footballer.
But Arnold had other ideas.
He wanted to be a body-builder.
When he was 15 he read about
the Mr Universe competition in a magazine.
He wanted to go to the America
that he saw on TV at school.
He started to dream and to work.
He skipped school to go to the gym
to build his muscles.

3 The Austrian Army

When Arnold was 18, he joined
the Austrian army as a tank driver.
He joined up so that he could eat fresh meat
to help his body-building.
After only one month Arnold ran away
to take part in a body-building competition.
He won but the army sent him to jail
for running away.

When Arnold left the army
he also left Austria.
He was free at last, to follow his dream.

4   **Mr Universe**

Arnold won the Mr Universe competition
when he was 20 years old.
He went on to win it six more times
and many other competitions as well.
In 1968, he went to America
for competitions, and he stayed.
Arnold became the world's
greatest body-builder.
He called himself the Austrian Oak.

The competition money was not wasted.
He started a bricklaying firm
with his friend.
Then he went to university
and got a degree in Business Studies.
Before he was 22 years old
Arnold was a millionaire businessman.

Arnold strikes a pose.

5   'I'll be Back'

For the next seven years,
Arnold lived the American dream.
He wrote body-building books
using the name 'Arnold Strong'.
The books were sold by mail order.
He got richer and richer.
By 1977, he was living
in a $200,000 home in LA.

Nineteen seventy-seven
was an important year for Arnold.
He started dating Maria.
She was the niece of John F. Kennedy
and part of a rich and famous American family.
He also started a second career.
He starred as himself
in the film *Pumping Iron*.
It was a film about body-building
and it made Arnold a household name.

Arnold on a date with Maria.

But it was the 1981 film,
Conan The Barbarian,
that made Arnold into a star.
The film is set in the time of legends.
It was made in Spain
and it took 20 weeks to shoot.
It was hard work for Arnold.
He was attacked by wolves,
kicked by a camel and run over by horses.
But the film was a big hit.
It made $100 million.

In September 1983,
Arnold became an American citizen.
It was a very important day for him.
For the ceremony
he wore a blue and white suit,
with a red tie and stars on his handkerchief.

The second *Conan* film
was not as successful as the first.
He needed to find a new kind of film.

Arnold got the chance with *Terminator*.
He was asked to play the human hero
or the killer cyborg.
He chose to play the cyborg,
who is the terminator.
In the film, the terminator
travels from the future.
His job is to kill a woman
to change the future.
Arnold had to train for three months
before filming started.
He trained to use
all the different weapons in the film.

Arnold didn't expect
Terminator to be a big hit.
It was made with only $6 million.
He had only 74 words in the film.
But three of them were:
'I'll be back.'
This phrase became his trade mark.
The film was a blockbuster.
Arnold became a Hollywood superstar.

Arnold as the Terminator in the hit film.

6   The Wedding

In 1985, Arnold carried an engagement ring
in his pocket for six months.
He was waiting for the right time
to ask Maria to marry him.
He found it in Austria.
Arnold and Maria were on holiday.
They were boating on a lake
when Arnold asked Maria to marry him.
She said, 'Yes.'

They were married in April 1986
in front of 500 friends and family.
There was lots of food and dancing
and a 2-metre tall wedding cake.
After the honeymoon
Arnold and Maria moved to their new house.
It cost $2.8 million and
is on the coast near LA.

Arnold and Maria on their wedding day in 1986.

7 Box-office Success

Arnold has always been a joker.
But his films didn't give him a chance
to be funny.
That all changed in 1988.
He was asked to star in the film *Twins*
with Danny DeVito.
They play test-tube twins
who are very different.
Arnold is over 6 ft tall
and Danny is very short.
People were surprised to see Arnold
in a comedy film.
But it was a box-office hit across the world.

Arnold with Danny DeVito in the box-office hit, *Twins*.

In 1989, Arnold was in Mexico
filming *Total Recall*.
Maria came to see him.
She told him to take time off in December.
When he asked why, she told him
that he was going to be a father.
Arnold was very, very happy.

He finished filming *Total Recall*.
In the film Arnold plays a builder
whose memory has been changed.
But he finds out that he's really
a fighter in the civil war on Mars.
So he goes back to Mars to win the war.
This sci-fi action film
was yet another Arnold blockbuster.

8 Family Life

After filming, Arnold took time
off to be at the birth of his daughter.
They called her Katherine.
Arnold turned down parts in two films
to be with his daughter.
He was happy to get up in the night
to feed her and play with her.
The papers called him
'Conan the Babysitter'.
But it didn't worry him – he was happy.

Arnold and Maria
went on to have three more children –
another girl and two boys.

After becoming a dad,
Arnold acted in another comedy,
this time with a class of little kids.
In *Kindergarten Cop* he plays a cop
who goes undercover as a teacher,
to track down some crooks.

Some of the best parts of the film
are when the cop tries to teach the class.
He is like a fish out of water.
Arnold was paid $12 million for the film.
It was a hit at the box office in 1991.

9 'Hasta la vista, baby'

Arnold's second film in 1991
came out in July.
It was a risk because it was a sequel.
Sequels are often not as good
as the first film.
Terminator 2 had to be different.

This time there were two terminators.
One good and one bad.
Arnold played the good one.
They both came from the future again.
One has to kill a boy, and
the other has to save him.
This time the film cost
$100 million to make.
But it was a massive hit.
We also had another of Arnold's
famous one-liners from this film.
This time it was 'Hasta la vista, baby.'

For the next six years,
Arnold's films were flops.
They made very little money.
But that didn't stop him.
He opened restaurants.
In 1992, he started the Planet Hollywood chain
with Sly Stallone and Bruce Willis.
He also started a production company.
It was called Oak Production.
He kept the American dream going.
He was the first civilian
to own the new American army jeep.
It was called the 'hum vee'.
This is short for 'High Mobility Multi-purpose
Wheeled Vehicle'.
It cost him $45,000.

Arnold was in another flop in 1997.
He played Mr Freeze
in *Batman and Robin*.
Mr Freeze planned to freeze the world
and leave it to the plants.
The film made some money at the box office.
But the critics didn't like it.

In the middle of filming,
Arnold had a pain in his chest.
He had to go into hospital
for a heart operation.
After the operation,
he took two years off work
to get better.

Arnold's latest films have included
End of Days and *The Sixth Day*.
Most of Arnold's latest films
have not made a big profit
at the box office.

But he will be back with *Terminator 3*.
This time he might be up against
a female terminator!

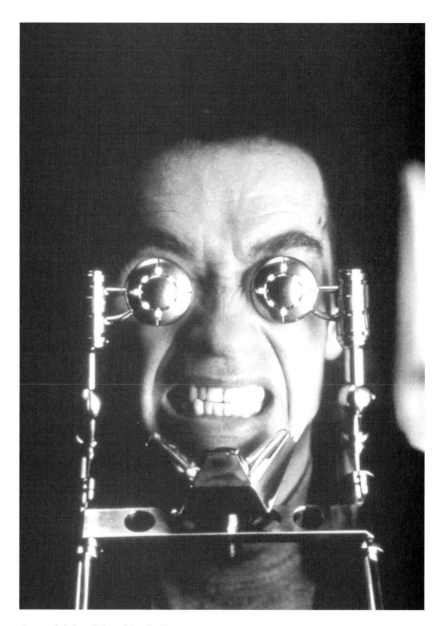

Arnold in *The Sixth Day*.

10 The Future

Whatever happens,
Arnold is still a king in Hollywood.
He has his business and his charity work.
Some say he'll go into politics.

His friends say,
'Whatever you think he is,
he's always something else.'

In other words:
he'll be back.

Arnold with Sylvester Stallone, Bruce Willis and Demi Moore at Planet Hollywood in New York.

Arnold's Films

Pumping Iron 1977

Conan the Barbarian 1981

Twins 1988

The Terminator 1984

Total Recall 1990

Kindergarten Cop 1991

Terminator 2: Judgment Day 1991

Last Action Hero 1993

True Lies 1994

Junior 1994

Eraser 1996

Batman and Robin 1997

End of Days 1999

The Sixth Day 2000